Coloring book for adults and kids amazing Crocodile image for design

This coloring book is belongs to

____

____

____

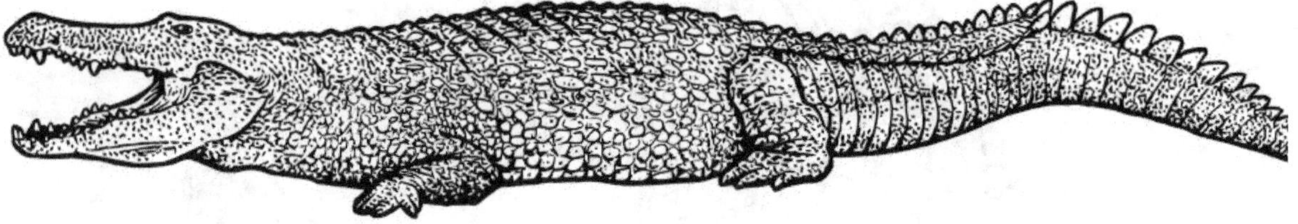

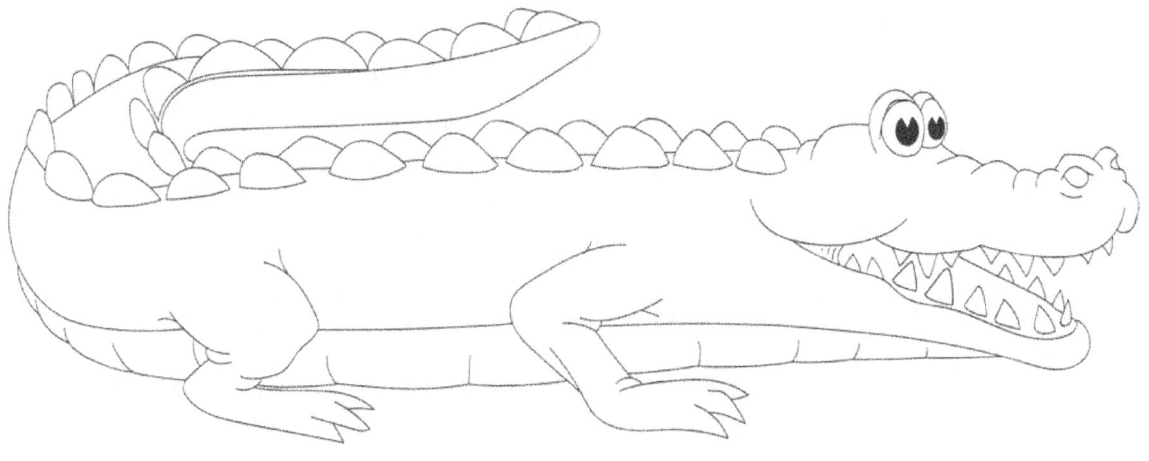

A a

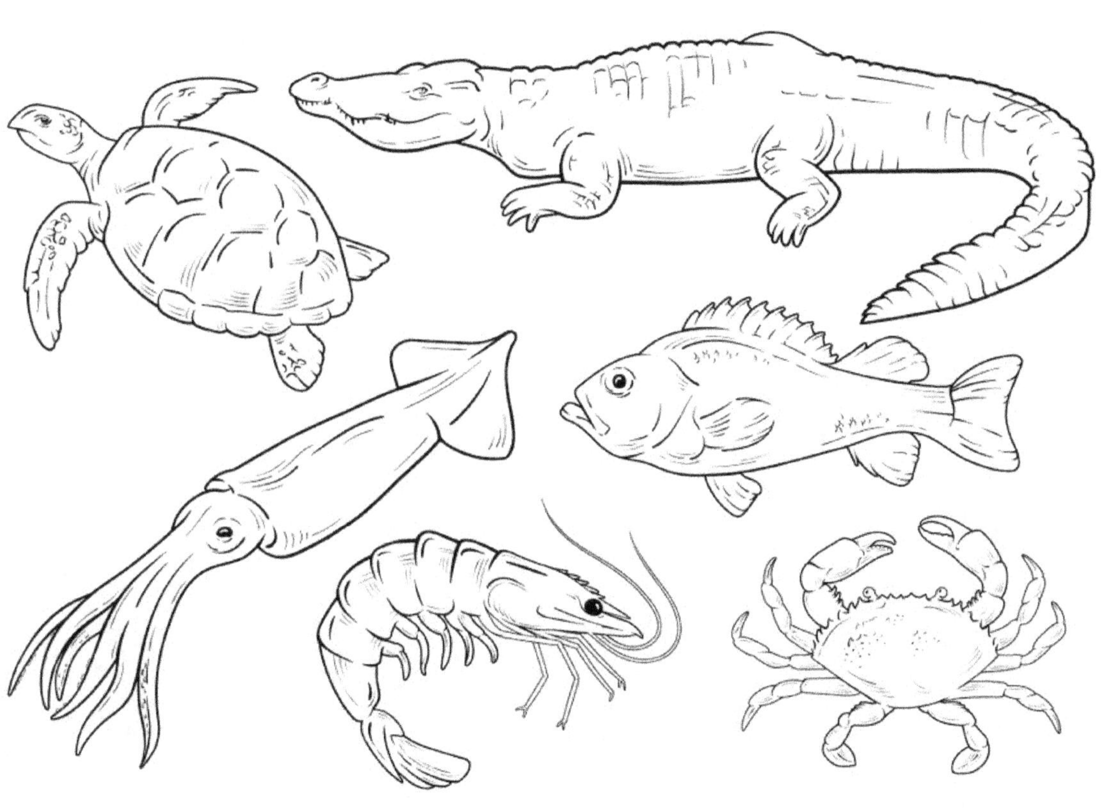

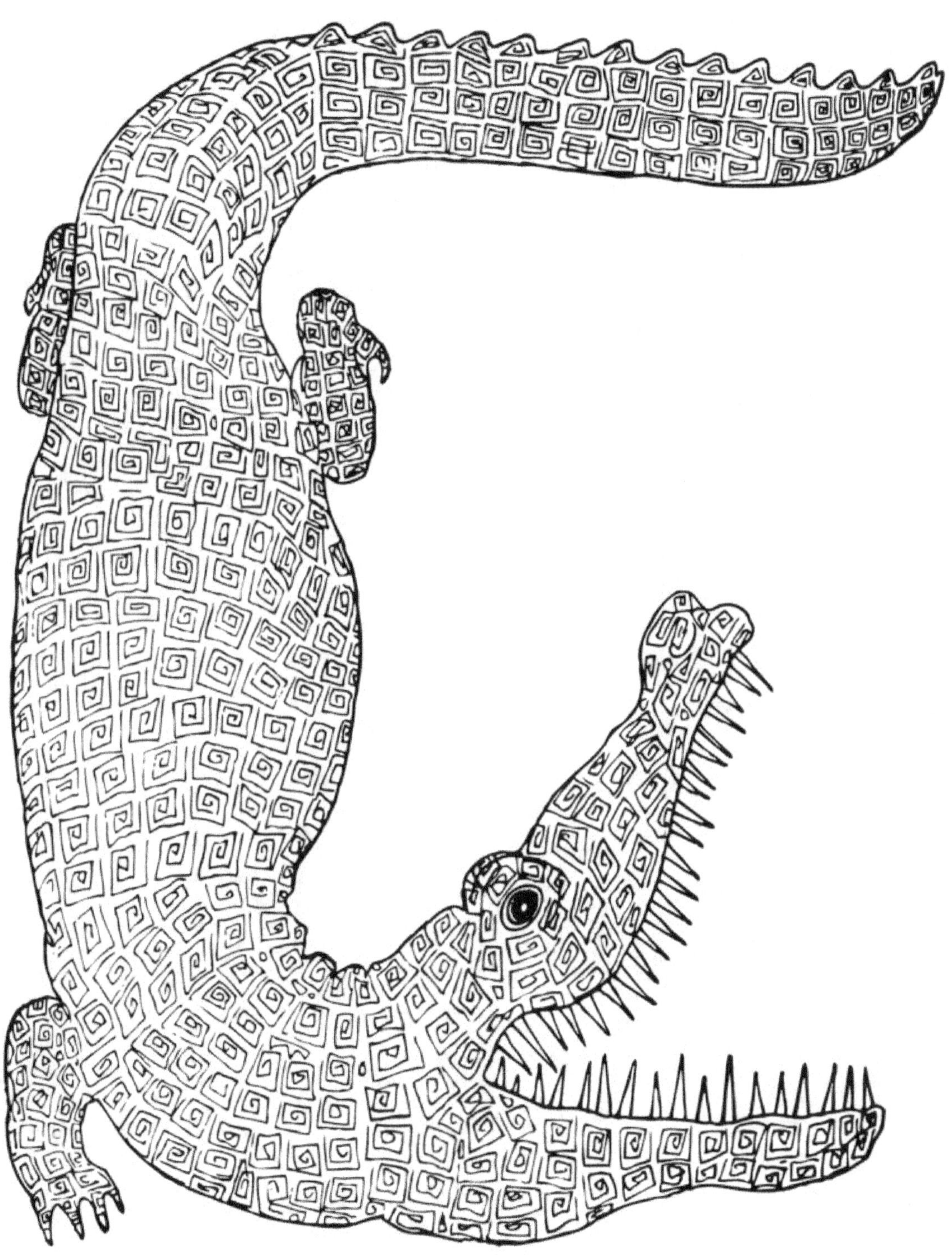

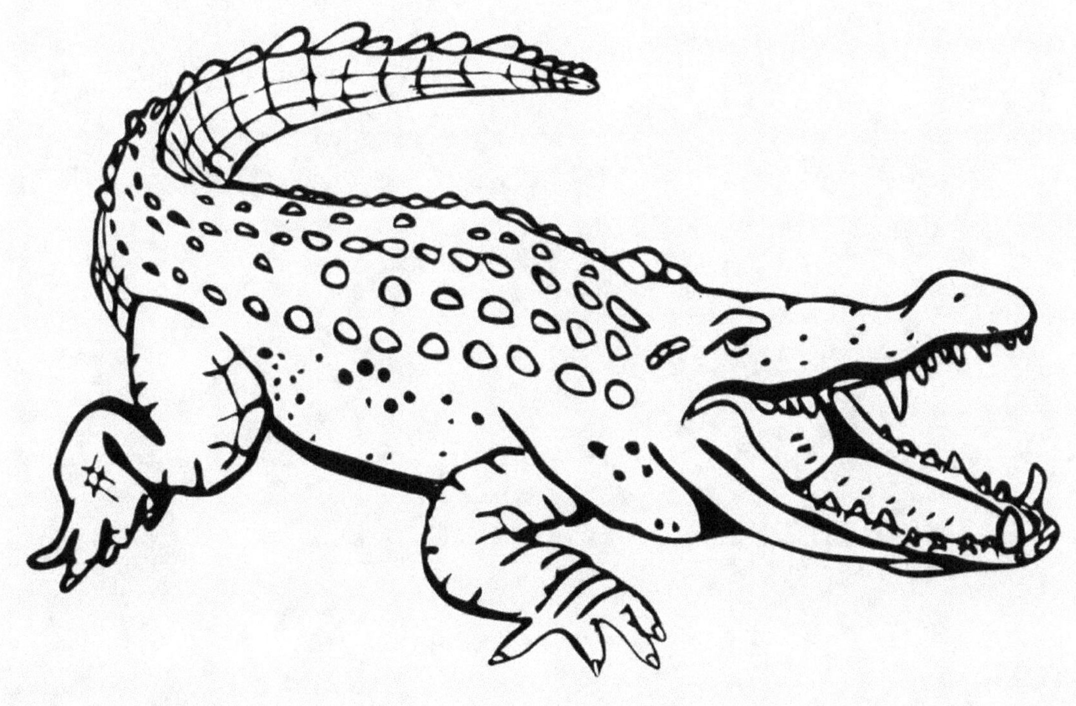

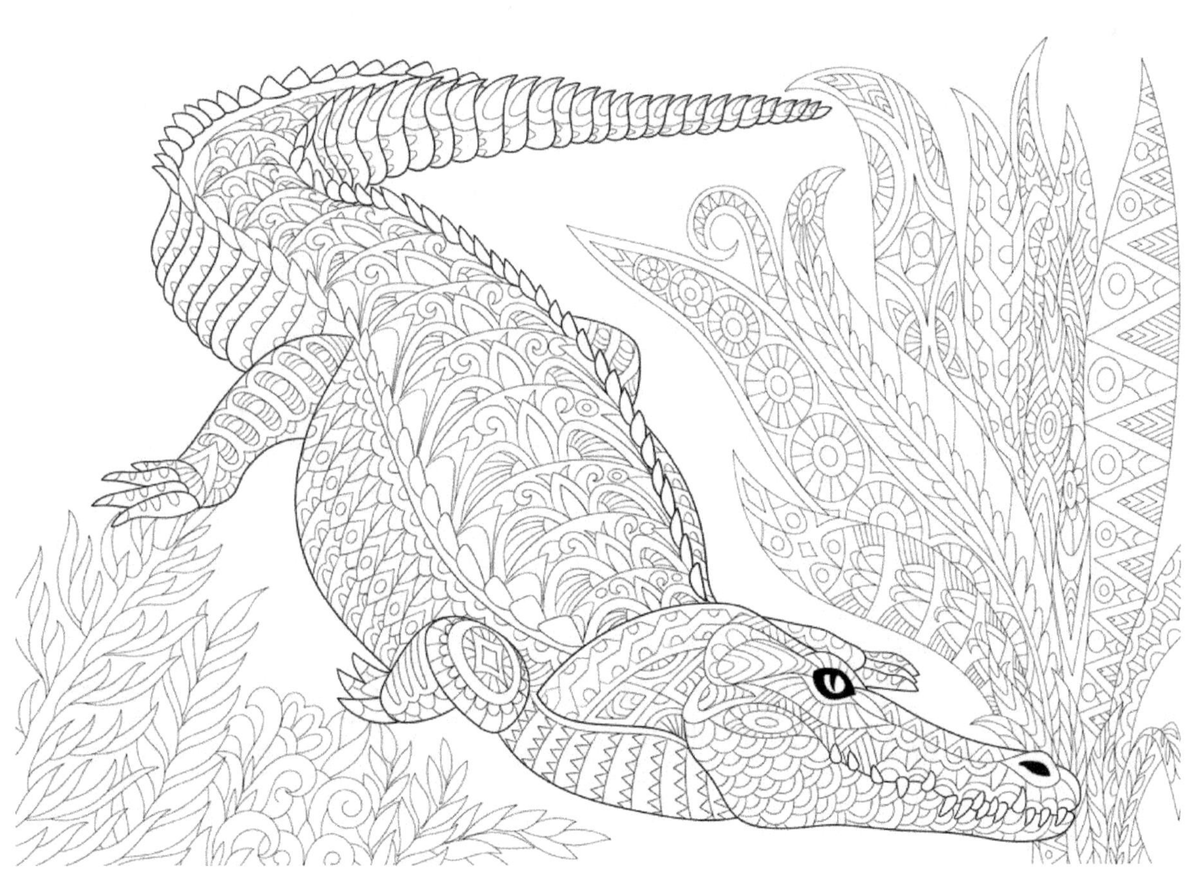

www.ingramcontent.com/pod-product-compliance
Lightning Source LLC
Chambersburg PA
CBHW081243250726

48654CB00012B/1466